Born and Not Wanted

Laura Veasey Williams

Bloomington, IN  Milton Keynes, UK
authorHOUSE®

AuthorHouse™
1663 Liberty Drive, Suite 200
Bloomington, IN 47403
www.authorhouse.com
Phone: 1-800-839-8640

First published by AuthorHouse 10/23/2007

ISBN: 978-1-4259-8837-1 (sc)

Library of Congress Control Number: 2007900096

Printed in the United States of America
Bloomington, Indiana

This book is printed on acid-free paper.

Table of Contents

Acknowledgements

The author wishes to express her sincere appreciation to her mom for sharing the history of her life. Her courage to withstand all discrimination, trials and dilemmas, prompted me to want to preserve it all through word. She taught not only me, but each of her eleven children by her way of life, that anything can be accomplished if we trust in God and continue to work toward success. I can not recall a night, before her retiring, in my entire life, that she did not open (her) King James Version of the Holy Bible for spiritual food. She read it in it's entirety many times over. It was placed in her casket by her youngest daughter upon her death.

Comfort and Peace momma, until we meet again.

I also express my deepest appreciation to my son, Kirk, for his encouragement and allowing me to digress from the attention given him during the initial writing of this novel. He was but a child at the time. As an adult, I continue to feel his support.

Thanks to Marshall E. Kuykendall for a copy of the only existing picture of my grandfather.

Preface

This is a true story. The story had to be told. I owe it to my family to do so. However, because my mother was so protective of the people who raised her and those family members that she came in contact with in her growing up, I owe it to her to use fictitious names to protect those whom she protected her entire adult life. Frankly, she was ashamed of the way that she was born into this world. She never spoke of it or even shared it with her children until they became adults. How different it would have been had she been born in the century in which we now live.

One of my cousins, who is truly a historian, as is my son, will be very disappointed that I did not use the correct names in the book. But I am sure that he can name every one mentioned as he reads. Not many adults or children, for that matter, could not recall the stories in history of these my family members, if the names were printed. They were quite well known.

Putting this story to pen and paper gave me pure gratification as I reminisced and remembered the mother, who battled discrimination, confusion, and loneliness, as she grew into the courageous woman, who told to me, the story of her upbringing. Not that she did not have a grandma and grandpa fighting right along with her. But they could only fight so long. Then because of the color of her skin she was on her own.

My mother being so grateful and kind toward others and her devout belief in God, allowed her determination, perseverance, direction and strength to conquer many struggles that she encountered.

Imagine a child born into a rich white family; white father, black mother, in the 1800's being raised by her white grandparents. Then thrust into a poor black world at seventeen to make a life for herself. What life? She had a life. Come along with me as the story unravels. Interesting. . . .

Laura Veasey Williams

1. A Child is Born

Everyone on the grounds, once a plantation, was moving busily, especially in the huts used to house black workers. Smaller children were scampering at play with no knowledge of the sincere chores being carried out by their mothers and older sisters. They were scurrying around, boiling water, tearing and boiling huge white cloths, and hanging them to dry. The men and boys were making themselves busy by carrying twigs to replenish the fires under the huge black pots that held the cloth and lye water.

After the men's chores had been completed, they gathered under a huge tree nearby, humming and singing in low voices. The women later joined them. A squealing scream was heard—silence fell over the entire area as women sprang to their feet, men laid down their fiddles, and scampering children became very still and quiet in wonder.

Then came the cry of a newborn. The silence lasted until an old black servant came to the door of the hut, holding a small bundle in her arms, smiling and nodding with approval.

"A girl!" she blurted out.

As she moved from the doorway back into the hut, the fiddles began to play louder than before. Yelps of happiness rang out, and there was clapping and dancing to the music.

After a while, those waiting patiently outside the hut were admitted inside. They left, a few at a time. The humming of an old, tired, and worn voice was heard. Everyone recognized the voice as that of Lucy, a servant who had worked on the Kahn ranch for many years, but this time, the sound was serene and pleasant, with a touch of happiness.

An hour or so later, down the road leading to the huts came a wagon, pulled by two high-stepping, shiny black horses. On the driver's seat was a well-dressed, clean-cut gentleman, sporting shiny boots, a cowboy hat, and a string tie.

A little middle-aged lady was seated quietly beside him. Her hair, beginning to turn gray at the temples, was pulled up into a ball on top. She held her hands firmly in her lap. Her black high-necked dress matched the gentleman's black suit.

They were Wiley and Susan Kahn, the owners of the ranch. The Kahns didn't believe in slaves. They paid wages to their servants for a good days work; however, fairly charging them for room and board at the end of the work week.

The wagon came to a halt in front of the newcomer's hut. Lucy, wearing a long dress adorned with a long white apron, appeared in the doorway with the bundle in her arms. She walked from the hut out to the wagon where the lady and gentleman were waiting.

The Kahn's youngest son, Isaac, was believed to be the father of the black servant Minnie's child. Minnie was Lucy's second child. Lucy pulled back one section of the cloth from the bundle she held in her arms. The gentleman looked down and so did the lady.

"That's Isaac's baby, all right," said the lady in a soft voice.

"It sure is," answered the man.

Lucy turned and went back into the hut. The wagon turned and went back down the dusty road.

Inside the hut, a pretty black girl with small features, tiny hands, and black, nappy hair that was pulled to both sides of her head in two balls just above her ears, lay awaiting the return of her child.

"What did they say, Momma?"

The woman placed the infant in her arms, saying, "They say it's Isaac's baby, all right."

The girl looked down at her baby with tears in her eyes and snuggled it close to her as she closed her eyes. Minnie, the mother of the infant, worked on the Kahn ranch, as did her mother, Lucy.

Wiley Kahn's forefathers had come to America on the Mayflower and his grandfather and uncles crossed the Colorado River in the early 1800s into territory now known as Texas, with the Father of Texas, Stephen F. Austin. History claims Grandpa Kahn, as well as, two of his brothers, as three of the First Five Texans. The Kahn's were treated almost as badly as slaves when they arrived. They weren't accepted by the American whites because many of their beliefs weren't in accordance with theirs. They even had to eat in the kitchens with the slaves.

Wiley's mother was Scottish and his father was Irish. He had one brother, Lawrence. Their mother died some years after their arrival and their father remarried. To that union was born one daughter, Sally.

After Wiley and his brother were older, their father went on a business trip to Austin, Texas, but never returned. It was believed that he'd been killed by Indians. The stepmother remarried and Lawrence later was killed in the Civil War. His younger sister disappeared, and it was never known what became of her. His father's brother, Ben, took Wiley in to raise him. Wiley later also went to war. Upon returning home, be began working as trail boss for Jack Peppers, a 6'5" Irishman who had moved to Texas from Little Compton, R.I. to take up ranching. And take up ranching he did by amassing thousands and thousands of acres of land, as well as, thousands of herds of cattle. Peppers was such a raskle it was hard to imagine him sharing the same bloodline with a former president and a renowned New England Poet, Henry W. Longfellow.

Peppers had a pretty sister, Susan, that Wiley admired for her soft speech and quiet gestures. As time advanced, Wiley asked Peppers for Susan's hand in marriage. He'd feared doing that, but finally worked up enough courage to do so.

Literally trembling in his shoes, Wiley went up to the house after payday one afternoon and knocked on the door. A loud "come in"came from the inside. Holding the doorknob for a spell, Wiley finally mustered enough courage to turn it. As he walked in, Peppers was seated at a desk with pen and paper.

Looking up, he said, "What can I do for you, Wiley?"

"Well, sir—" Wiley started.

Peppers, getting impatient, said in a strong voice, "Yes, Wiley?"

Wiley continued, "Since I've been working for you here as trail boss, I've saved quite a bit of money and, and," he stuttered a bit, and then went on, "I'd like to take myself a wife."

Peppers blurted out, "And who have you chosen as the lucky bride, Wiley?"

"Well, you see, sir," he said, wondering if he shouldn't forget the whole thing, but remembering that pretty little woman, blurted out, "with your permission, sir, I'd like to marry your sister, Susan."

Knowing Wiley was only seventeen, Peppers replied, "You can't take care of yourself, let alone a wife, Wiley Kahn."

"Oh, but I can, sir," Wiley insisted. He then stood as straight and tall as his weak legs would let him and said, "If I can care for your ranch as I have, I can take care of myself and a wife, sir." After a moment's hesitation, he added, "Don't you think, sir?"

Peppers smiled and consented, "Well, you sure can try, Wiley Kahn."

At that moment, Wiley let out a loud whoop-ee, jumped up, and clicked his heels.

Then he tactfully composed himself, cleared his throat, and walked over to Peppers, shaking his hand and saying, "Thank you, sir. I'll do my best to make Susan very happy."

Wiley was so happy that he went straight to town that afternoon. Upon returning, he was so intoxicated that he fell off his horse, flat on his face, as he came through the gate. The ranch hands' laughter and teasing remarks lured Susan and Jack from the house. There Wiley lay, as drunk as a snake that had fallen into a barrel of whiskey, head bobbling and falling time and time again in his effort to retrieve his small, frail body from the dust.

Jack Peppers' laughter was louder than anyone as he looked at Susan and said, "Is that what you want as a husband, a young drunk who can't even stay on his horse?"

Susan, obviously insulted, raised her brows as she momentarily stared at her brother, then at the ranch hands. Then, grabbing her long dress with its many underskirts, she rushed into the house as fast as she could, slammed the door, and waited with crossed arms for what she knew was sure to come.

"Here you go, little darlin', let ole Shole help you," said one of the hands.

"Need some help, Shole?" said another.

"Let me go," were the words through all the laughter and commotion that Susan recognized as Wiley's.

Splash was the sound she'd been waiting for. They'd dumped poor Wiley in a water-filled trough. Soon the laughter ceased and all was quiet.

Susan Peppers became Mrs. Wiley Kahn the next month. They had eleven children, with none of them living to reach adulthood but the last three—Gilbert, Isaac, and Etta. Most were lost in childbirth, while others reached the ages of six months, three years, and similar ages.

Susan Kahn, was a Yankee and never believed in owning slaves, and after her marriage to Wiley, his uncle Ben disowned him.

Susan and Wiley's oldest surviving son, Gilbert, had four children—Maxine, Delores, Billy, and Abe. Etta had only one child, Wynette, and Isaac was the father of the servant's little bundle, the only child he ever had, for when the child was born, his parents turned him out. He had disgraced the family and had to leave the ranch and live on his own. He was raising cattle up in the panhandle and died of pneumonia about a year later, in 1896.

1856-1963

Lorraine's Black Grandma, Lucy Norris

2. The Night Ride

A long black carriage, moving very slowly pulled by six black horses, was leaving the cemetery grounds, followed by several covered buggies. Sobs of distress and hurt were heard, as well as cries of "Momma, Momma." An older woman was doing her best to comfort four small children—Pearl, Grace, Able, and Johnny. Their father, Joe Peppers, Jack and Susan's brother, was sitting in a daze, seeming not to hear or see much of anything.

Finally, looking up and taking the smallest child in his arms, he said, "I'll take care of you, my child. Don't cry. Momma wants you to be a big boy. Daddy'll take care of you. I will. I must."

A day or two after the burial of his wife, Joe Peppers went to his servant's quarters and knocked on the door. Lucy answered.

"Come in, Mr. Joe," she said.

"Lucy, I must have someone in the house to care for my children. A man can only do so much. Bring your husband, Charlie, and take the large room next to the kitchen."

"But, Mr. Joe," said Lucy, "My chillun won't have nobody to take care of them if I gotta live in the big house."

"Lucy, you may bring your youngest, but that's all, only the youngest," he said as he started walking back to the house.

Lucy went back in and sat down, head hung low.

"What the hell am I sposta do with my chillun, throw them away?"

"Things will work out, Lucy," Charlie assured her.

Lucy and Charlie had three children, Susan, Minnie, and Leola. Susan had been wanting to be married for some time and went ahead with her plans. Joe's sister and her husband, Susan and Wiley Kahn, took Minnie, their second child, who was nine years old, to live with them, and Lucy and Charlie, along with their youngest, moved into the big house.

Some three years later, Joe Peppers took himself a wife. Everything went wrong then, for Lucy, that is. As Joe and Mrs. Peppers were seated in the sitting room one afternoon after supper, Lucy could hear them talking.

"Joe," demanded the new Mrs. Peppers, "I think you should tell the children that they may come to me now if they need anything." Joe continued to read the paper as she continued, "Oh, I know they've been used to going to Lucy, but that's because they had no one else to go to. Besides, it'll help us to get better acquainted, don't you think?"

Joe looked up momentarily, then became interested in his paper again.

She paused for a moment and then continued, "I'll begin to leave a list of household chores each day I'd like for Lucy to perform. Oh, and a list of things that I want her to cook for each meal."

Lucy could see Mr. Peppers from where she stood in the kitchen, nodding his head every once in a while to assure Mrs. Peppers that he was still listening, but she wasn't sure he was listening at all, because before long he fell asleep, just as he'd always done after supper and a cup of tea. Lucy gave a devilish smile, as if she was glad he'd gone to sleep while his domineering wife was talking. She finished her chores in the kitchen and went to her quarters.

Eventually, the new Mrs. Peppers had a son for Joe Peppers, whose name was Josh. Charlie and Lucy were becoming tired of the new Mrs. Peppers' demands and decided to leave.

"Mr. Joe," said Lucy one day as she was baking and he'd come in, as usual, to talk.

"Yes, Lucy?"

"Must be nice to have a wife round the house again," Lucy said with a smile.

"You betcha, Lucy. Mrs. Peppers has been a real help to me," he said.

"Then you don't need me no more, do ya?" said Lucy bluntly.

"Oh, Lucy!" said Joe. "Sure I need you. I don't know what I would have done without you for the past three years."

"But what about these past few months?" she questioned. "You've been very helpful to Mrs. Peppers and me, and the children—" he said, searching for words.

Joe looked up and said, "Lucy, I know it's been hard for you to get used to Mrs. Peppers, since you've run things around here for so long, but you'll get used to each other as time goes on."

"Well, you see, Mr. Joe, Charlie and me talked it over and we think since you have a woman 'round the house now, well, we thought we'd go work for Ms. Susan and Mr. Wiley, being that's where my child, Minnie is, and my brothers, Rob and Thotoe, is too."

"Well, Lucy, if that's what you want, but I sure will miss you and Charlie. The children will miss you, too."

"They's big enough to look after their selves now. Not that I won't miss them little rascals, though."

"How soon do you want to leave?" Joe said.

Lucy replied, "I'll stay till Mrs. Peppers is able to get around and care for herself and the baby."

"Good enough," said Joe. Tasting Lucy's cake dough with the end of his finger, he began to walk away, then turned and said, "Thanks for everything, Lucy. You're a jewel."

"Get outta here, Mr. Joe, 'fore there's tears in the cake dough," said Lucy while shooing him with her hand.

Minnie, who was a teenager, worked in the big house, cleaning and cooking. The Kahns were having dinner. Gilbert, their oldest son, had married and gone, but Isaac, the second son, and Etta remained. Minnie had served them all and was waiting patiently beside the dining room door leading to the kitchen to see if she could be of further assistance.

Isaac gulped his food down as if he hadn't eaten in days.

"I'll have some more potatoes, Minnie," he said.

Minnie got the bowl and served him again. As she did, Isaac watched her intensely, as though she was bringing him a pot of gold. She again took her place beside the door. Isaac ate slowly this time, staring at Minnie between bites.

Minnie, feeling rather uncomfortable, asked, "Ms. Susan, Mr. Wiley, will that be all for now?"

"Yes, Minnie, thank you," said Susan.

"Lovely dinner, Minnie," complimented Wiley as he relaxed in his chair and lit a cigar.

Minnie quietly left the room.

As Minnie prepared water for the dishes, she heard Isaac excuse himself, saying, "It's a lovely night out. I think I'll take a ride."

"All right, Isaac," said his father.

Isaac was nineteen, six foot two inches tall, with large muscular shoulders, blue eyes, and dark hair, and he looked as stately as a Roman warrior when he rode a horse. When he returned, Minnie was walking from the big house to the servants' quarters.

Isaac rode slowly up to her and asked, "Minnie, would you like to go for a ride?"

"No thanks, Mr. Isaac. I'd better get to the house. Momma'll be looking for me soon."

"Soon, but not right now," he quipped as he reached down and swooped her off her feet, riding away again. She struggled to free herself, but with no success, since he was very strong.

It was an experience she'd never before encountered. She was frightened of her mom and dad finding out, or Mr. Wiley and Ms. Susan, for Isaac had prompted her never to tell anyone, that he cared for her and thought she was beautiful.

Minnie was somewhat uncomfortable after that whenever Isaac was around, for she could see him watching her every move. She sensed that Wiley felt something, because he'd try to rush Isaac off to his chores whenever he was hanging around the kitchen area where Minnie worked.

Minnie was humming one day as she was washing dishes, which was unusual, for she was a quiet person, when she suddenly felt the warmth of a figure behind her. Before she could turn, large, strong arms slipped around her waist. She turned, seeing that it was Isaac, being careful not to scream, for Wiley was in his study, and if he knew of Isaac's behavior, he'd surely be punished. He might even send her away to be with people she knew nothing about. Isaac held her close and tight against him. She struggled to get loose, but soon calmed down, rather enjoying the warmth of his body against hers as he kissed her lightly on the mouth. He then gave a laugh and went out the door.

Minnie began feeling sick several weeks after her night ride. When she got up in the mornings to go to the kitchen to prepare breakfast, she could hardly dress, due to the fainty feelings and nausea. She could manage her chores fairly well on the morning side, and then the sickness would disappear. That lasted about two months.

One afternoon, after dinner had been served and the dishes washed, Minnie decided to give the kitchen a good mopping. She'd finished half the floor when everything before her began to move. She remembered nothing else. When she opened her eyes, standing over her were her mother and father and Uncle Thotoe. She'd been placed on a cot in her mother's room.

"What happened, child?" Lucy asked.

"I don't know, Momma. My legs jes went out from under me."

"How?" Lucy demanded.

"I was mopping," was her reply, not volunteering information unless she was asked.

"You feeling that way now?" continued her mom.

"No, Momma," she answered

"Felt that way before?" Lucy's questions not letting up.

"Sometimes."

"Tell me, child, when you feel that way again. You nearly scared your poor momma to death," Lucy said, putting an end to the questions.

"OK, Momma."

A few days later, Isaac saw Minnie sitting on the porch.

He walked over and said, "Feeling better now, Minnie?"

"Yeah."

"You sure are pretty, Minnie," commented Isaac.

"Don't say that to me."

"Why?"

"'Cause."

"'Cause what?"

"'Cause I'm a servant," Minnie complained.

"Ha, Ha, don't make you stop being pretty 'cause you're a servant," he said admiringly.

Minnie sat very still. Then he noticed tears trinkling down her cheeks.

"What's the matter?" asked Isaac.

She didn't answer, looking down and picking at her nails.

"I guess you're mad at me for hurting you," Isaac said, offering an explanation.

She still didn't answer.

Isaac pleaded, "Well, stop crying. I won't do it again, I promise."

"Don't much matter now," she sighed. "I'm gonna have a baby."

"Have a what?"

"A baby."

"How do you know?"

"Jackie just had a baby 'bout two months ago. She said she did just like me before her baby was born."

"Boy, are we in trouble!" exclaimed Isaac.

"No, you're in trouble. I'm gonna tell my momma and poppa, and then I guess Mr. Wiley's gonna send me away."

"Don't tell them just yet, Minnie."

"I have to. I can't keep my belly hid forever. My clothes are too tight now, and sooner or later, Momma's gonna notice, anyway. Many babies she helped bring into this world."

Minnie turned, wiped her eyes on her apron, and went inside. Sure enough, she was becoming rather plump, especially in her midsection.

3. Lucy Breaks the News to the Kahns

Lucy rose early the next morning, even before Minnie got up, dressed, and sat in her rocker thinking, "I gotta tell Ms. Susan and Mr. Wiley, and tell them if that boy, Isaac, don't keep away from my Minnie, I'm gonna knock him in the head or somethin'. She ain't nothing but a baby herself, and now she's gonna have a baby. But they's good people, and they'll do the best for my Minnie. I guess she can go stay with her sister, Susan, till the baby comes."

While Lucy was lost in her thoughts, Minnie had awakened, put on her clothes, and was getting ready to leave.

Lucy looked up and said, "No, Minnie, you stay here till I talk with Ms. Susan and Mr. Wiley."

Running and falling around her momma's neck, Minnie said, "I'm sorry, Momma, to put you to this trouble."

"Not your fault, child. It's that son-of-a-Kahn they's raising that caused all the stink. I'll be back in a minute."

Lucy, with beige dress to her ankles, long white apron, hair neatly plaited, white stockings, and black laced-up shoes, walked out the door, down the steps, and down the dusty road to the big house.

Minnie, not knowing what to do with herself, sat in her momma's rocker and rocked a while, then hopped up and stood at the window and watched her poppa, who always got up at dawn, chopping in the fields alongside Aunt Sarah and Uncle Thotoe. Becoming more impatient, she went out onto the porch and sat on the steps.

"I hope Momma hurries back," she thought. "Sure is lonesome here with nothing to do, 'specially when I don't know what's going on up there. I guess I'll have to leave this place. Sure hate to, though. It's the only home I know."

Then she just sat there, not thinking of anything in particular, until she heard her momma say, "Minnie, go on up there and fix breakfast."

There was a short pause, then Minnie jumped to her feet, standing very straight, her eyes wide open.

Lucy, realizing that Minnie wanted to hear more, said, "Mr. Wiley hit the ceiling.

He gonna send Isaac away."

"Send Isaac away? But I thought—"

"Isaac told his pa he wanted to work around here and earn wages to take care of his baby, and boy, that's when the ceiling flew off, for sure. Mr. Wiley say he better not see him nowheres 'round you at no time." Pausing and looking down, Lucy continued with a chuckle, " Hee , Hee, 'magine a white boy wantin' to take care of his black baby."

She quickly changed her grin to a frown and said, "Won't have to send him nowheres, if he jes' let ole Lucy get her hands on him." Looking up, she told Minnie, slapping her on the rear end with an upward stroke, "Now you get, and stay away from that boy, ya hear me?"

Minnie, walking swiftly, at almost a trot set off by the slap on the rear, looked back over her shoulder and said, "Yes, Momma."

Still, she couldn't help thinking of her momma's words with every step she took (send Isaac away, send Isaac away) until she reached the big house.

Several months passed, with Minnie gaining weight by the day. It was getting difficult for her to keep on schedule, because she couldn't move as swiftly as she had before. She never saw Isaac around, though, only from a distance. When meals were served, she had to fix his plate and leave it covered on the stove to keep warm. Someone must have been taking it to him someplace, for he never ate at the table with the family anymore. However, it was easy to stay in that house and not see anyone, for the Kahn house was three stories high, with a sun room that was used as a reading room on top. There was decking on all three levels. Susan loved to sit outside while she sewed and knitted in the afternoons in her rocking chair.

Susan came into the kitchen one day, and seeing Minnie moving more slowly than ever, said, "Minnie, you look a little tired and I think you could use some rest. Tell your Aunt Sarah to take your place in the house until after the baby comes."

"Oh, but Ms. Susan, I feel fine," pleaded Minnie.

"Minnie, please do as I say."

Minnie looked down, as if ashamed of her condition, and replied, "Yes, Ms. Susan."

Susan was a sympathetic, kind, gentle lady who never raised her voice. She loved to sew and sewed beautifully. She got joy from buying bolts of material and sewing them into dresses, pants, and shirts for the poor—it mattered not to her whether white or black. After making the garments, she'd get into her carriage and ride around to different houses to distribute them. The recipients may have had almost all of their clothes made from the same fabric, but oh did they love to see her coming. The children would run out to meet her and run alongside the horses or attach their bodies to the carriage and get a ride until they reached their houses. God bless the soul of that kind little ole lady—never to die.

Isaac (1876-1896), Lorraine's Father

4. Isaac's Departure

The child, a little girl, born on a November day in 1895 to the servant Minnie, was one month old on the day Isaac was to leave. He'd seen his child one afternoon, but no one knew about it but Minnie and him. She thought it only fair to let him see her, and took the baby out to the barn when no one was around and she'd seen Isaac go in. He thought she was a beautiful little girl.

"Please tell her about her daddy some day, will you, Minnie? I wish things were different somehow and I could watch her grow up." After holding and admiring the baby for a few minutes, he said, "You'd better go back now. I've caused enough trouble as it is."

Minnie felt sorry that Isaac had to leave his home and couldn't help but wonder, "Why are they sending him away and not me?"

She wanted to cry, but said, "OK, Isaac, I'll tell her."

Then she went back into the house.

Isaac's dad had spoken to a man that was passing through on a cattle drive about taking Isaac on. He paid good wages and gave his men meals. Minnie was watching from the porch as Isaac was preparing to leave. She'd just fed the baby, who was taking her afternoon nap. All the servants were standing around. Uncle Thotoe was shining Isaac's saddle and currying his horse. Susan and Aunt Sarah were seeing that a good lunch basket was prepared in the kitchen for the journey.

When all was finished, Susan came out and gave Isaac a black leather billfold and said, "This should keep you going until you earn your first month's wages."

She kissed him on the cheek, held him tightly around the waist for a while, and then backed off. Etta was sitting on his horse as Thotoe led him to where Isaac was standing. Sarah handed him the basket, which he strapped onto the side of his horse.

Wiley walked up, shook hands briskly, and said, "If you have any trouble and need help, you know where to find us."

Etta slid off the horse, catching Isaac's neck as she came down, giving him a big hug.

He set her on the ground, giving her a swat on the rump and saying, "You be good, Etta."

He climbed onto his horse, gave him a kick in the ribs, and rode swiftly away with dust flying from the hooves of the horse as he rode.

Susan walked over to the porch where Minnie was standing and said, "You bring the child and move into the house on the left wing, Minnie. We've prepared quarters for you there."

"Yes, Ms. Susan," she replied.

The Kahns preferred their servants not answering them with, "Yes, ma'am" or "No, ma'am." Instead, they instructed them to answer with, "Yes, Ms. Susan" or "No, Mr. Wiley."

Everything was moving smoothly when, after about a year, a fast rider came onto the grounds.

Seeing Thotoe near the barn, he rode up and asked, "Is this the Kahn ranch?"

"Yes, sir," replied Thotoe.

"Where might I find Mr. Kahn?"

"He's up to the big house, sir," Thotoe said, pointing as he answered.

"Thank you."

The rider, looking as if he'd been riding for days, approached the house, got off his horse, and knocked on the door. Thotoe saw Minnie let him in. Shortly thereafter, Wiley came out onto the porch.

Seeing Rob, he said, "Rob, go and get everyone. Tell them to come quickly." Turning back toward the house, Wiley added, "Minnie, see to Ms. Susan. She'll need comforting. Isaac has passed away."

"Oh, my god, Mr. Wiley!" exclaimed Minnie, feeling as though her heart would stop beating any minute.

She grabbed little Lorraine, who was toddling nearby, and went upstairs as fast
as she could.

When the servants reached the house, they all gathered round the porch, where Mr. Wiley was standing. They could tell that something was wrong and that he was very disturbed.

"Isaac," he paused a while, then continued, "my son, has died of pneumonia."

"Good heavens."

"God help him."

"Oh, my!"

Various other cries were also heard throughout the group.

Wiley, standing very straight and composing himself, continued, "He was on a cattle drive up in the panhandle."

Everyone was very quiet, other than some sobbing from the older women who had cared for him during his childhood.

"I'll be leaving in the morning to bring his body home. Thotoe, see that my wagon is hitched and ready by sunrise. Rob, I'd like you to come along. I'll expect all of you to carry on as usual until I return. Lucy, Ms. Susan might like for you to stay close by while I'm away. She's very disturbed." He paused for a while with head hung, and then said, "And so am I."

He then turned and went back into the house, where Minnie was standing just inside the door.

"Minnie, will you see that the gentleman has some food and a hot bath? I'd like my breakfast very early in the morning."

"Yes, Mr. Wiley."

Minnie went to the edge of the porch, gave the baby to Lucy, and went inside, busying herself warming leftovers and getting towels and linens from the linen closet. She could hear the servants humming, followed by a soft and beautiful song. It was their way of mourning Isaac's death and comforting the family.

Early the next morning, Wiley and the gentleman, with Rob on the driver's seat, horses tied to the back, pulled out in one of the wagons covered with a dark canopy.

"Leaving on such a journey must be heartbreaking," thought Minnie. "To disown and send your son away, then have him return within a year, only to place his cold body into the cold, cold, ground and cover it forever."

The Kahns were never able to talk about Isaac again. Had they felt responsible for his death? Had they felt guilt? Was it just the deep love they'd had for him during the nineteen years they'd had him? Devastating—

Lorraine, Age 5

5. The Little Dickens

Lorraine was about five years old, and what a spoiled little dickens she was.

That's how Susan, her grandma, always referred to her when she'd done something wrong. Being the only child on the place, Lorraine got lots of attention.

Etta had gone to boarding school, and only the servants and Mr. and Mrs. Kahn were on the place. Little Lorraine was Mr. Kahn's pride and joy. Each evening when he came in from his work on the ranch, he in his chair and Susan doing some handwork on her sewing while seated in the sitting room, Lorraine would run and jump into his lap.

He'd say, "Whose baby are you?"

"I'm your baby," she'd reply.

"You're not. You're Minnie's baby."

"I'm not. I'm your baby."

"Minnie, come and get this gal," he'd call.

Once, when Minnie came for her, Lorraine caught him by the neck and bit his ear.

Later, in would come Uncle Joe, Mrs. Kahn's brother. Being on a nearby ranch made it possible for him to visit almost every day. He was a tall, stout man. He'd slip out of his shoes to relax for a while as tea was being served each evening after supper.

After nodding a spell, he'd wake up and yell, "Lorraine! Come here, baby, and put your Uncle Joe's shoes on."

She'd run in and tug with his shoes until she finally got them on his feet.

"Now hug Uncle Joe's neck," he'd say.

She'd jump up around his neck and give him a big hug, then would go to the door along with her grandma and grandpa to see him off. Then she'd piddle around one place and then another until it was time for bed.

As soon as Mr. and Mrs. Kahn had gone to bed and gotten settled, there would be the sound of a pit, pit, pit, coming toward their bedroom.

Almost too small to be seen from the high bed, Lorraine would say, "I wanna sleep with you, Grandma,"

Her mother, missing her, would call, "Lorraine."

At that instant, she'd run as fast as she could, tug at the covers, and say, "No! Get me, Grandpa, get me."

Then he'd reach down and pull her in, always in the nick of time.

"She's all right, Minnie," Mrs. Kahn would call.

Minnie, coming to the door, would say, "I don't see that you can sleep very well with her in there. She won't be still."

"Don't you want to sleep with your momma, baby?" Susan would ask.

"No," very sharply was her answer. "I wanna sleep with you."

"Well, if you're not very still, I must make you get up and sleep with Momma," her grandma would say.

Minnie would then turn, shaking her head as she went back to her room.

Lorraine would be very still for a few minutes, but then she'd put one foot on her grandpa and her head right under her grandma. A short time later, she'd move her whole body very snuggly under her grandpa. Nothing was said. Maybe she was asleep, they thought, but all of a sudden, she'd swiftly turn over to snuggle under her grandma.

"All right, pest your little time, I'm going to put you at the foot of the bed if you can't be still," her grandma would warn.

Then Lorraine would lay very still with her eyes shut tightly, touching neither of them, until she'd prop one foot on her grandma and one on her grandpa. Mrs. Kahn would then get up and pull the covers up from the foot of the bed. The little pest, knowing very well what that meant, would then crawl down there as her grandma covered her snuggly. There she'd sleep all night.

6. Minnie Marries

One afternoon after dinner was finished and Minnie had served the Kahns tea in the sitting room, Susan noticed Minnie still standing there, not saying a word.

"Yes, Minnie, what is it?" said Susan in her soft voice.

"Ms. Susan, Mr. Wiley," Minnie replied, addressing them both as she turned to one, then the other.

She paused until Wiley blurted out, "Yes?" as he sat forward in his chair.

"Kopey, who works over on the Blair's ranch," Minnie said, swallowing and twiddling with the end of her apron, "and comes over to visit me sometimes—"

"Yes, I remember him," said Susan.

"Well, he wants me and him to be married," Minnie finally gets out, as if it was the hardest chore she'd ever encountered.

"And you want to know how we feel about it?" Susan said, trying to help a bit.

"Yes, Ms. Susan," Minnie said, looking up in relief.

"Will you be leaving us?" Susan asked.

"No, Ms. Susan. You see, after we marry, Kopey would like to work for you and Mr. Wiley."

Susan looked at Wiley and smiled.

"I think that can be arranged, Minnie," Wiley said with assurance, sitting back in his chair.

Minnie relaxed a bit, letting her apron fall into place, and noticing what she'd been doing, patted it down.

"I hope that you and Kopey will be very happy, Minnie," said Susan.

"Thank you, Ms. Susan," said Minnie, very pleased.

"Tell Kopey to come in within a few days and talk with me, Minnie," Wiley said.

"Yes, Mr. Wiley."

Susan added, "After you're married, Minnie, you can no longer occupy the east wing, but you and Kopey may have the cabin next to your parents."

"Yes, Ms. Susan."

Minnie turned to leave, then turned to them once again, saying, "Thank you both."

A smile from them both was her answer.

Minnie took Lorraine a few days before her day to be married and moved to the cabin she'd been given. The cabin was small, but very cozy. From the porch, she could walk into a small sitting room with a couch, two chairs, and a corner table with a lamp. That, along with the front porch, covered one entire side of the cabin. Directly to the right were two rooms. The one in front had a double iron bed, a dresser with kerosene lamps on either side, a wash table with washbowl and pitcher, and a chair. The room in back only had a small cot, a rocker, a large trunk for storage, a wash table, and a tin tub in the corner. That was the room

Lorraine was to occupy. The wooden floors were scattered with multi-colored rugs, and small potbelly iron stoves in both rooms. The place was brightened by colorful curtains throughout, made by Susan, of course.

After Minnie and Kopey were married, Kopey moved in and started working for the Kahns. Lorraine loved her daddy. She'd swing on his back and sit on his lap. Anytime he was standing, she had him around his legs. Kopey tried to avoid Lorraine as much as possible. He didn't seem to like children and never showed any love for Lorraine.

"Minnie, can't Lorraine stay with Lucy and Charlie now?" he asked one day.

"No, Kopey, she's my baby. Her place is with me."

Minnie told Kopey about Lorraine's father, how he had died, and how the Kahns had treated Lorraine as one of the family. Lorraine even ate all of her meals at the table with them. The Kahns were grand people. Many would have marked Lorraine's birth off as just another one of those things, but not them. They held on to the memory of their son, Isaac, through his only child, Lorraine.

Susan missed the little dickens when Minnie moved into her own cabin. She didn't see as much of Lorraine as she used to. Whenever she saw Lorraine playing outside, she'd take time to watch for a while.

Kopey was raking leaves one afternoon and Lorraine was playing around the pile he'd made.

He continually warned her, "Get back, Lorraine, get back."

He then took some matches from his shirt pocket, lit the pile all around the edges, and as it flamed up, he took Lorraine by the arms and swung her again and again over the flames as she screamed for dear life.

Susan ran out and yelled, "Kopey, you're a mean and cruel man to take a little innocent child and swing her over an open fire. You get off my property, and don't ever come back."

Minnie, hearing the commotion, came running, saying, "Ms. Susan. Kopey is my husband and if he leaves, I must go with him."

"Do as you wish, Minnie, but you leave that child here. No man as mean and cruel as that has any business around children."

The day Minnie and Kopey were to leave, Susan sent one of the servants to bring Lorraine's things to the big house. She'd prepared a little cot for her with a quilt and pillow right beside their bed. Minnie had asked Lucy to look after Lorraine, because Susan wouldn't allow her to take her. But not one night did she stay with Grandma Lucy and Grandpa Charlie. She never fretted about Momma Minnie, either, who Lorraine never saw much and who died at an early age from diabetes. The little dickens was where she loved to be, with Grandma and Grandpa Kahn.

(About twenty years later)

After Minnie and Kopey left, Kopey got into a fight with a white man and killed him with a singletree. Kopey was sent to prison. He later tried to get away. They tracked him with dogs. When he reached a river, he had run so long that he gave out. As he attempted to cross the river, there was a white man and woman in a boat with a child. He caught onto the side of their boat, trying to hold on. The man hit Kopey in the head with the oar and stunned him. Kopey then swam until he reached the other side. As he tried to climb a tree, the dogs caught him and tore him to pieces before the guards could get across the river. Minnie grieved and grieved over Kopey's death and died shortly thereafter.

7. Lorraine Finds out About Color

Lorraine grew up not even giving a thought about color, because it was never discussed or mentioned around the Kahn ranch, but she soon began to learn. She traveled a lot with the Kahns, always going into hotels with them, until they went to San Francisco.

The manager admitted them, then looked down at Lorraine and said, "You can't bring a nigger in here, but she can stay out back with the servants if you'd like."

Mrs. Kahn grabbed a piece of her luggage in one hand, Lorraine's hand with the other, and snapped, "She'll do no such thing!"

She started toward the door and Mr. Kahn followed, gathering the rest of their baggage. They went back to the train station, where they sat all night, just to keep Lorraine with them.

Mrs. Kahn decided to hire a tutor for the children. Gilbert lived nearby and had four children. Etta had come back to live with her parents, and had one child. During the time she was in boarding school, she disappeared for about two months before the Kahns located her. When she was found, she was married. The marriage lasted about four years. Her husband was a very rich businessman who was quite a bit older. She soon decided that she couldn't live with him and while helping him count his money at different times, she'd roll up large bills and stick them into her long, thick hair until she'd saved enough to leave.

The first tutor was a young, pretty woman, Harriett Seymore, from Boston. She taught the children all winter, Lorraine included, and returned home in the summer. That lasted about three years, until Harriet married. Then came Mrs. Johnson. She treated Lorraine like the rest of the children for about six months, then began to ignore her, never explaining anything to her or helping her in any way. Lorraine had to learn whatever she could while Mrs. Johnson explained things to the other children. Mrs. Johnson was soon dismissed.

Grandma Kahn made Lorraine the prettiest little dresses, as she did for the other children, curled her hair, and dressed her for church. One Sunday in particular, so proud of her dress and her long beautiful curls, Lorraine ran down to the kitchen to show the help. She loved those people and spent a lot of her time with them.

One of the workers looked at her and said, "You think you're white, don't you? Well, you're not. You're black, just like us. Can't you see that your skin isn't the color of those white folks' skin?"

By that time, her grandma had called for her and they were ready to go. Lorraine was very quiet on the way to church, and after they got there, she kept her head hung. When she looked down at her hands, she tried to hide them in the ruffles of her dress.

Grandma Kahn sensed that something was wrong and leaned over and asked in a whisper, "What's wrong, baby?"

"Nothing," she replied softly.

When they returned home and had eaten dinner, Mrs. Kahn asked Lorraine to come to her bedroom. She put Lorraine's little red rocker in front of her big chair and sat down.

Lorraine came in, sat down, and looked up at her grandma, who began the conversation by saying, "You know we don't have secrets that we keep from each other and we don't tell each other stories. Now, tell me, baby, what is it that's bothering you?"

"Grandma, Callie said that I think I'm white but I'm not," she said, "She said I was black, just like her. Why is my skin darker that yours?"

"Now, baby, when the world was very wicked, a long time ago, God destroyed the world by letting it rain forty days and forty nights. He told Noah to build an ark and to save a pair of every kind of animal on the Earth. An ark is a houseboat that can float on water. He put a girl and boy deer, a girl and boy horse, bird, goat, and a girl and boy of every other kind of animal that we have on this Earth on the ark."

"Did he put a girl and boy sheep on there, too, Grandma?"

"Yes, he put two sheep on there, too, and he also put three of his sons and their wives on the ark. When the rains came, it made it flood, and everything outside the ark died. After the waters subsided and everything had drowned, the ark landed between two mountains. Noah came out first and as he walked around, he found a grapevine loaded with grapes. He was so happy that he and his family were saved, he made wine from the grapes and drank too much. One of his sons, Hamm, laughed at him. The other two sons took a cloth and walked backward and covered their father's nakedness, for he'd somehow pulled his clothes off. Noah fell asleep. When he awakened, he told Hamm that for making fun of him and his nakedness, all of his children would be born black. That's why your skin is darker than mine. But don't feel bad and worry about what Callie said, because we're all first cousins."

Lorraine felt some better, but began to notice the difference (which was very little) in the color of her skin and that of Delores, Maxine, Billy, and Abe, whom she played with, rode horseback with, slept with, and was tutored with every day of her life.

Poor little angel, to think of her trying to cope with a problem such as that at such a young age—a problem that's difficult for grownups even today. But her Grandma and Grandpa Kahn made it as easy for her as they possibly could. I can see why she loved them so much. They were such good people.

Grandma Lucy had an older sister who worked for Mr. Kahn's brother, who had disinherited him when he married Susan. When she got too old to work, he put her out and she had no place to go. Yes, you guessed it. Wiley went and got her and let her stay on his place until she died. He'd go out, look in on her, and cry and talk about how his uncle had worked that poor old soul all of her life, and now that she was of no more good, he'd put her out. The Kahns had kind hearts, saw no color, and helped anyone in any way that they could.

Susan always relished that they'd gotten what they had from hard work, with no help from anyone, and that they could enjoy and dispose of it any way they pleased. She could do the work of any man and then run the household, which she did for many years. Little Lorraine grew up very much in her grandma's image.

8. Lorraine Has Her Way

Lorraine loved to ride horseback and was very good at it. She was a trick rider. She could ride standing, hand-standing, hit the ground and back to the saddle, go under the horse's belly while moving, and jump barrels. There was a contest in town every year, and she longed to compete.

She and her cousins rode and raced right down the middle of town all the time, as kids often did. Some of the citizens couldn't conceive of a black girl riding straight through town on horseback.

One day, as they were riding, a man standing nearby yelled, "Nigger, you get out of these streets on that horse and go out on the prairie somewhere and ride."

"I don't have to," replied Lorraine, who was about twelve years old now. "I can ride down these streets any time I please."

"No, you can't," he yelled, "and if I see you up here again, I'm going to break your galdurn neck."

Lorraine and her cousins rode once again through that street, just as fast as their horses would carry them, and back again. Then they went straight back to the ranch and Lorraine told Grandpa

Kahn what the man had said—excluding, of course, that they had aggravated him by riding back down the street again.

Grandpa Kahn went out to the stables, saddled his horse, and said, "Come on, Lorraine, we have business in town."

He climbed up and rode out, with Lorraine riding right beside him. When they reached town, the man was sitting on a bench in front of the dry goods store and Lorraine pointed him out.

"Mr. Buck," Wiley yelled as he rode right up to him, "I'd like to have a word with you!" The man raised his head to listen as Wiley continued, "Did you see this little nigger ride through here on this black horse?"

"Sure did," he answered, and proceeded to tell him his side of the story, adding, "then she rode down the street and back again, just to show me that she could."

"Well, you see, Mr. Buck," Grandpa Kahn said, "This little nigger is *my* little nigger, and she can ride down these damn streets as much as she damn pleases, and if anyone as much as lays a hand on her, they're going to answer to me. Good day, Mr. Buck."

Lorraine rode back beside her grandpa at a slow trot, thinking, "He sure did take up for me. Now I can ride down the town streets any time I damn please."

And she did.

Lorraine loved horses and loved to ride them. Before her dad died, he had bought three horses and had saved $1,000, all of which was given to Lorraine when she was older. The races and stunt riding show was coming up and Lorraine planned to enter. She, her grandma and grandpa, and the cousins all went into town. It was a big day for the people in the area. Lorraine walked up to sign up for the events.

"Sorry, but you can't sign up for the races," the man said.

Her grandpa, hearing him, stepped in once again.

"She'll sign up or there won't be any races here today."

Lorraine was immediately given a number and asked her name. Her grandpa was a wealthy rancher and respected by all. She won first place in the races.

Where would it end? Would she always be protected by those fine old people?

What would happen to her when they're gone? Time would tell.

Mrs. Kahn, foreseeing that Lorraine needed to learn to take care of herself, enrolled her in public school after they moved to Beeville, Texas when Lorraine was twelve. When she was home, she saw to it that Lorraine learned to sew by asking her to assist her at different times.

When Mrs. Kahn was to have a dinner party, she'd tell Lorraine, "I'm going to dress you up real pretty and put a little white apron on you. I'd like for you to help me serve our guests."

She'd coach Lorraine as to which side to stand on, what to serve first, and how to be polite. Of course, her grandma was helping, as well. She also showed her how to set the table until eventually she was able to do all of it alone. It was her way of trying to teach Lorraine a trade or vocation so she could one day take care of herself.

After Beeville, Mr. and Mrs. Kahn bought a cottage in San Marcos, on the corner of San Antonia and Samanchez. Before that, they traveled to Newark and Salt Lake City. They were beginning to get feeble and had more and more trouble getting Lorraine into hotels. Mr. John and Etta had separated and she and her child, Wynette, were living with them again.

Etta and Lorraine once had differences and she slapped Lorraine in the face. Lorraine caught her by the legs and dragged her from upstairs completely to the bottom of the stairs. After two years, the Kahns decided to get rid of that place, but they didn't know what to do with Lorraine, who was approaching seventeen.

9. Lorraine Leaves the Kahns

It was beginning to be difficult for the Kahns to travel with Lorraine because she was quite a large girl and hotels wouldn't admit her. Her grandparents were beginning to get old and needed rest when they traveled and there were layovers, so when a friend of Mrs. Kahn's asked if Lorraine could come and work for her and her husband, Mrs. Kahn agreed.

Did her grandparents feel as if they'd done enough for her? Had they kept her that long because they felt responsible for her birth, or did they really accept her as their grandchild?

All of the other children finished high school and went on to college, but Lorraine never went any farther than the seventh grade. Can't you just feel the hurt she must have felt when all of her friends and cousins went off to college, but she couldn't go?

The woman of the house where Lorraine was working expected her to take care of a sixteen-room house, cook, wash, and iron. Never having cooked a meal in her life, washed clothes, or ironed, Lorraine was lost. She had, however, kept her own room, so she was familiar with cleaning. She could sew and serve dinner, but nothing else.

Lorraine did the best she could, for she wanted to please her grandma, who'd been so kind to her all those years. The family was the Johnsons. Mr. Johnson was the postmaster of San Marcos. They had a son who was a lawyer and a son in law school. She agreed to pay Lorraine $15 a month. The first month passed very slowly, then she was paid.

Lorraine decided one day, "Shoot, I don't have to do this. These people didn't raise me. I don't owe them a thing. I'm going to find Grandma Lucy and Grandpa Charlie."

After the children were all gone and the Kahns became older, they didn't need as much help, so Lucy and Charlie left. They went way out on a rice farm in Bay City, Texas, to work. Upon finding them, Lorraine was told that it was no place for a young girl—nothing but a lot of rice farm workers, and no entertainment at all. They let her stay a few days, and then told her to go to stay with her cousins in town. When she arrived, they were about to move to Galveston, Texas, and insisted that she come with them.

Mrs. Kahn had left money with Lorraine, for fear that she'd need more than her first month's salary. Things went well with Lorraine and her cousins—as long as she had money.

When the rent was due, it was, "You pay it, Lorraine, and we'll give it back."

When they went to the grocery store, they said, "You buy, since you're not paying any rent."

You guessed it. She was never paid back and was treated coldly when her money played out. She decided to leave, for she'd

48

found employment with Mrs. Jones as a dishwasher at Hogan's boardinghouse. She later became head waitress. Isn't God good, taking care of a lonely child on her own for the first time with no place to really call home?

While working at Hogan's in Galveston, Lorraine met a young man. He was very handsome, well-dressed, with black hair, and blue eyes. His mother was a Louisiana Frenchman and his father was a white man, like Lorraine's. He kept asking her out, but she refused. She had several lady friends that she'd go out to eat with and take in a movie on her nights off.

The young man, Godfrey, found out when and where she and her friends went to the movies and began to go himself. Then he'd ask if he could walk her and her friends home. That went on for several months. Lorraine had been telling an older lady friend that she stopped to talk with on her way home from work in the afternoon about Godfrey. It was that woman who persuaded Lorraine to let him date her, so she did.

Later, Godfrey asked Lorraine to marry him.

"Marry him?" she thought. "I don't need a husband. I'm fine just as I am."

Again, the older lady offered advice, saying, "Baby, you're a nice girl. This world is so hard and dangerous to be in all alone. Why don't you accept? Then you'll have a companion—someone to look after you."

Lorraine thought and thought about it, and on April 15, 1912, at 6:00 p.m., she and Godfrey Veance became man and wife. A string orchestra played the wedding march and highlighted the dinner after the wedding. It was the beginning of a full childbearing, hardworking, sometimes happy, but most times sad, life for Lorraine Kahn Veance—a life that was to be entirely different from the one she had experienced in childhood. A transition from a rich, white life to a poor, black one.

Lorraine and her husband.

10. Many Tragedies

About a year and a half after her marriage, Lorraine gave birth to her first child, a girl named Sheryl. A year later, a boy was born who died at birth. Two years later, a son, Godfrey, Jr., arrived, and on and on, until she'd given birth to twelve children.

When their first child was very young, the family was in the 1914 storm in Galveston, Texas, which destroyed almost everything they had. A year after that, a fourth child, Randy, was born. In 1920, their home was destroyed by fire. Lorraine had left the three children asleep in the house while she went out back to milk the cow. The oldest boy woke up and woke the other two as he got out of bed.

The little girl kept complaining, "It's cold, Bubba. It's cold in here."

Bubba, as she called him, almost five years old, decided to put more wood on the fire. Godfrey had cut the wood into fine strips so it would easily catch and would be easy to handle. As Bubba stuck the wood in the iron stove, it immediately flamed up, frightening him. He then jerked it out again, throwing it back into the wood box, which caused the other wood to catch fire.

A young girl in the neighborhood was passing, saw the flames, and ran out back to tell Lorraine, "Mrs. Veance, your house is on fire!"

"Oh, my god, my babies are in there!" yelled Lorraine, throwing the bucket of milk aside and running into the house as fast as she could.

In the meantime, neighbors had gotten the children from the porch, where they'd gone when they'd been frightened by the fire. Lorraine ran in, frantically looking for the children, not knowing they were outside. She collapsed inside from inhaling too much smoke.

Godfrey was coming in on his motorcycle, excited, frantic, and as usual, drove under the house to park. The houses in Galveston were built very high because of the many floods the island encountered. The floor fell in on him and knocked him unconscious. Someone had called the fire department and the firemen came in time to get Lorraine out of the burning house and to drag Godfrey from the debris under the house. Lorraine was revived and told that her children were all right, but Godfrey was still unconscious. When he did open his eyes, he couldn't speak.

The fire had broken out at about 7:00 a.m., but all Godfrey did from that time until about 8:00 p.m. was scratch on a pad someone had given him when he tried to mumble something. It said, "Where are my babies?" When he was told the children were all safe, he seemed to relax.

That afternoon, an old woman who lived down the street and had heard what had happened came to Godfrey and had someone turn him over, face down. She massaged his spine vigorously from the nape of his neck to the tailbone, over and over again. Around 8:00, he moved on his own and spoke.

Lorraine began trying to locate her Grandma and Grandpa Kahn several hours after the fire was extinguished. She got no answer. When she did get in touch with them, there was more bad news. Grandpa Kahn had passed away that same day. Her grandma had been trying to reach her all day, but because of the fire, the phone was out.

Strength and faith, Lorraine. Hold on to it. God puts no more on us than we can bear. Easy to say, isn't it? Grandpa Kahn, a man she loved dearly, was gone, along with her home and everything in it. He'd been on a cattle drive and had contracted pneumonia, which was his cause of death.

Lorraine and her family were housed at one of their neighbors' homes while looking for a place to stay. A few days after talking to Lorraine, Grandma Kahn sent her a sewing machine, bolts of material, sheets, curtains, and kitchen utensils. Along with the things their neighbors gave them, they soon set up housekeeping again.

11. Lorraine Buys a Home

Godfrey came in one day and called, "Lorraine, Lorraine!"

Hearing him, she came to the bedroom, where he'd thrown a suitcase on the bed.

"Yes, Godfrey, what is it?"

"I have a job offer in San Antonio. It pays a lot more than I'm making here. In a year or so, we could have enough money saved to put a down payment on a house and get the kind of furniture you've always wanted."

Lorraine, astounded, stood without a word as she watched him gather his shirts, socks, and underwear from the drawers.

Finally she said, "When are you leaving?"

"Very early in the morning. I have to report by noon," he said. "Get my gray suit pressed while I go to the corner and have my shoes shined."

Godfrey reached for the door and started out, then leaned back in and said, "Oh! I want you and the children to stay with Momma while I'm gone, I've already arranged it."

Then he closed the door. Lorraine, still standing there, couldn't believe what had just transpired.

Trying to get everything together in her mind, she sat on the side of the bed and began to think, "He'll work in San Antonio. He's leaving in the morning. The kids and I will stay with his mother. His *mother*? Well, I won't interfere. Maybe things will work out all right."

She then got up and started looking for Godfrey's gray suit in the closet.

Early the next morning, Lorraine was up cooking breakfast and seeing that Godfrey hadn't forgotten anything he might need. He was to catch the 5:00 bus.

Before he left, he kissed the children, who were still asleep, and warned Lorraine, "Now remember, when the rent is due next week, you and the children are to move in with Momma. That will save a little money. I'll let you know where I can be reached as soon as I can."

Then he left. Lorraine didn't say a thing to change his mind, knowing very well that she and Godfrey's mother didn't get along.

She thought, "I'll do the best I can to get along and maybe we'll never have to do this again."

Lorraine and her three children had to stay in one room. Her mother-in-law was grumpy. She insisted that Lorraine do the cooking and buy the groceries, since they were living in her house. She also insisted that the children not be allowed to come into the other part of the house.

Godfrey came home one weekend with only $40 in his pocket. Lorraine, being very disappointed, tried to look on the bright side of things.

"Well, I'll take what he has and get a few thing the kids have been needing for a long time," she thought.

Godfrey's mother began to grumble right after his arrival about having to take care of his family for him and that he hadn't sent her anything for her troubles. Godfrey was eventually as fed up as Lorraine and reached into his pocket, giving her all of the money he had, except his fare back to San Antonio.

About a month after Godfrey had returned to San Antonio, Lorraine received a letter from him. It read: "Work here is not as good as I had expected. I'm ready to come home. Please send my fare. I'll see you and the children in a few days. Godfrey."

Lorraine immediately went to the post office and sent Godfrey enough money to get home. She wanted her family together again. Three days passed, but no Godfrey. Then a week passed.

"Surely he'll be here by the weekend," she thought.

The weekend came and went. No Godfrey. Lorraine finally gave up and stopped looking for him.

About three weeks later, another letter from Godfrey came, asking for money to come home. She refused, not even answering the letter. He came home a few days later with only $4.00 in his pocket. How lucky could she get? How much could she stand? Where did she get her strength?

Lorraine's children were her only happiness.

She'd dress them in their Sunday clothes to go to church, stand back, take a good look and say, "Aren't they beautiful? These are my beautiful children."

Then, down the road she'd go, baby in arms and the toddlers behind.

Lorraine started working now as a cook for Lieutenant Maynard and his wife in the houses edging the Gulf of Mexico, in the East Beach area of Galveston. She was given one of the quarters to live in. Godfrey did the yard work. They were beginning to do reasonably well. Lorraine had been saving money to buy a house. She knew she was to get some money from Grandpa Kahn's death, but the estate hadn't been settled. She wanted a home of her own very badly. She'd been sending Godfrey to deposit money in the bank whenever they had anything to spare. Soon she'd have enough.

She was very happy these days. She'd been visiting furniture stores and had seen just the furniture she wanted.

Several months had passed since the tragic fire and the death of Lorraine's Grandpa Kahn, but in September 1920 came more sad news. It was a telegram from Aunt Etta, saying that Grandma Kahn had passed away and asking her to come. In her will, Grandma Kahn had left Lorraine $500, but she'd stipulated that it must be used toward the purchase of a home or she wouldn't get it.

After returning from the funeral and getting settled again, Lorraine and Godfrey set out looking for a place. They decided because of the storms in Galveston and the bad luck they'd encountered there that it would be best to leave and look for a place in a nearby town. They found a place in Dickinson, Texas, only two large rooms at the time, but on five and a half acres of land. The acreage was overgrown with tall grass and trees, but the location was on a main highway.

Lorraine thought, "We can clear the land and farm and still have a home."

Godfrey was against it. He could see nothing that could be done to that place, but Lorraine insisted. She'd finally found someplace she could call her own. A few weeks later, Grandpa Kahn's estate was settled. She received $500, which enabled her to buy her home.

"Now I have enough in the bank to get furniture just like I want," she thought.

She got the children dressed one day and went to the bank to get the money to pay the balance on her furniture. She'd already gone one day and given the gentleman at the furniture store a small sum to hold the furniture.

"Mrs. Beaver, I'd like to draw out $300, please. I've bought a home and I want to get my furniture. The man is holding it for me."

She went on and on as Mrs. Beaver was checking her account. Mrs. Beaver returned with a slip of paper in her hand.

"Honey," she said, "you only have $150 in the bank."

"Oh, no, Mrs. Beaver," Lorraine said, thinking she'd made a mistake. "I had $200 and then I sent $250 more about two weeks ago, $100 last week, and—"

"And," said Mrs. Beaver firmly, "Godfrey withdrew $100 last month, $75 two weeks later, and—"

By that time, Lorraine had shut out the conversation. All she heard was "you only have $150."

Godfrey had been keeping some of what Lorraine was sending to be deposited and withdrawing more at other times. Lorraine, holding tightly to her baby and clutching another child's hand while a third was holding on to her dress tail, flinched as her eyes filled with water.

"Yes, Mrs. Beaver, please let me have whatever's left."

On her way home, she felt as if the world had begun to rest its clouds on her very thin shoulders. She weighed no more than 125 pounds and was 5'9" tall. She was from a family of tall people. Now she'd have to settle for much cheaper furniture until she could do better. When she got home, she sat her babies down around her, cried harder than ever before, and prayed that God would look after she and her children, for she was trying as hard as she could to look after them herself with very little help from their father.

What was she thinking? Did she not want the feeling of abandonment again? Was she imaging the determination that her Grandma Kahn had when her grandpa went out on long cattle drives for months at the time and she had all the chores to do? Did it come from the African side that you survive from day to day, do as you're told, and move on? Did she truly believe that God would take care of it all and that she'd let him? Strong women— *S trong Women.*

Godfrey came in late that afternoon, as usual, saying, "Fix my supper. Is my bathwater ready? Where are my brown trousers?"

Boy, what gall.

Lorraine said, "Godfrey, I went down to the bank today to get the money to pay for the furniture. There was only $150." Godfrey stopped to listen, and she continued, "What did you do with it? Why did you get the money that we had for the furniture?"

He replied by saying, "You ought to bury your damn money if you don't want anyone to use it. I bet it on the horses."

In a rage, she flew into him, fighting and screaming, only to be left on the floor and alone with her children to cry and worry.

"I'll fix him," she thought. "I'll never again, as long as I live, let him know how much money I have or where it is."

Lorraine's Aunt

12. Lorraine Spies on Godfrey

The next night, Lorraine decided, "I'm going to find out where Godfrey goes every afternoon."

She asked a friend to come over and see to the children for a while. She dressed in one of his suits, put her hair under a hat, and went down on the boulevard where he usually went. It was beginning to get dark and no one noticed her. Godfrey and one of his friends were in conversation with two young women. They walked and giggled and talked for several blocks, not noticing Lorraine, who was walking slowly, always a few yards behind.

"Oh, Godfrey, you're a gas," one of the girls said.

"Hey, let's take in a movie," the other fellow said.

They all agreed, rushing toward a car parked nearby.

"So this is what he's doing while me and my babies sit at home alone," she thought. "I'll just leave him to his women and fun."

She went back home and went to bed, but couldn't help thinking, "What makes him do this? Why can't he be happy at home with us? We have such beautiful children. I keep the house clean. I cook what he likes, but he never has time for us."

She prayed, "Dear God, am I not wanted twice?"

About 3:00 a.m., Godfrey came tipping in, undressed, and eased into bed. Lorraine was watching every move, not being able to go to sleep.

When he settled into bed, she said, "What did you do tonight?"

"Oh, Joe and I walked around the beach a while, then got up a domino game with the other guys. Played damn near all night, didn't we?"

"Oh, Godfrey, you're a gas. Let's take in a movie," Lorraine blurted out.

"What?" Godfrey said, astonished. "Who do you have spying on me? I guess one of your boyfriends is keeping an eye on me to try to get you. Tell him to go to hell. I do what I want, when I want, and ain't a damn thing anybody can do about it."

A typical line. Well, she sure had enough time to have a boyfriend if she'd wanted one, but those words made her jump from the bed, crushed. She ran to the children's room, got into bed with them, crying and praying until she cried herself to sleep.

It was good that she believed in prayer. The only thing that could change that man was God.

It wasn't long before Lorraine received another $500, with which she paid the balance on her home. Grandma Kahn's estate had been settled. Had it not been for the kindness of those two old souls, she would not only have had a *hard* way to go, but a *harder* way to go. They were responsible for her having a home of her own, even if it was the proceeds from their deaths, for she would have exchanged the home she'd longed for, for so long, any day in exchange for their lives. She loved and missed them tremendously. However, her Aunt Etta stepped in, giving her support whenever possible. She was, however, reluctant because of Lorraine's husband and his worldly ways.

Lorraine was expecting again. Her fifth child, Frank, was to be born sometime in January. During her pregnancy, she continued to work. Godfrey was seldom home. He was beginning to stay away for days at the time. He came home one afternoon and told Lorraine that he'd asked his mother to come and stay with them until after the baby was born.

Great, another person for Lorraine to feed and take care of. Lorraine would have preferred that she didn't come, but always kind and looking at things optimistically, she told herself that even though he wasn't there most of the time, Godfrey must have been concerned about her and the children, to have asked his mother to come. - P l e a s e.

Pregnancy after pregnancy, baby after baby, she toiled, struggled, and kept going. Things were getting harder, if that was possible. Two more boys, Isaac (named after Lorraine's father) and Carl, and then the eighth child, Minnie, named after Lorraine's mother. Because the babies were born so close together, only two or three years apart, it was difficult to keep them in shoes, but Lorraine kept her children clean, they ate, and they all went to church, one behind the other—everyone but their dad, Godfrey.

Thanks to Grandma Kahn's teaching her to sew, she made dresses for the girls and shirts for the boys from the feed sacks after the cows and horses had devoured of their contents.

A couple of years later, her ninth child, Wynette, was born. Lorraine had to begin buying milk because her breasts were dry. There was a German man and his Italian wife living just a block up the road from Lorraine and Godfrey. She was having a child about the same time each year that Lorraine was, so she let Wynette feed from one breast as her baby fed from the other. They had a lot in common: babies almost every year, husbands who were mean to them, hard work, and a strong faith in God. They began visiting and sharing each other's burdens.

That family raised vegetables, chickens, and pigs, just as Lorraine and Godfrey did, and shared when the crops were ready for picking. The older children were responsible for planting and harvesting.

Lorraine wasn't completely forgotten by the family that had raised and nurtured her most of her life. Etta (Lorraine's dad's sister) continued to help whenever she could. Each Christmas and Easter, all the children stood on a piece of paper. Their feet were traced with a pencil and then cut out. *Boy* or *girl* was then written on the paper and sent to Etta.

A week or two later, Lorraine would receive a large box with shoes for every child in the family. Oh, the smiles that followed the opening of that box! Clothes from Etta's daughter, Wynette, and her daughters, Susanna and Jane, came every year. Lorraine would take them apart at the seams and cut them down to fit her children.

Wynette had married a wealthy oil man and had three children—two daughters and one son. She was also liberal in sending things to Lorraine, her first cousin. That lasted even after the twelfth child (her last), little Lorraine, named after her mother, was born in February 1939, exactly 100 years after the birth of Grandpa Kahn in 1839.

At different intervals, Etta would also come down and bring large boxes of badly needed canned goods, hams, and bacon slabs to tide them over. All of that was well and good, but, did Lorraine ever wonder why, being born to Etta's brother, she was so poor and struggled so hard because of the color of her skin while they were so rich and had everything? She never questioned it. Only God knew for sure.

Frankly, Lorraine was ashamed of the way she'd come into the world. She never spoke of it or complained. She never even shared her white life stories with her children until they were adults. She was so protective of the family that had gone out of their way to make her as comfortable as possible—under the circumstances.

13. Godfrey, Jr. Runs Away

Lorraine's older children were beginning to grow up. Godfrey was mean to the older boys. He left them to chop in the fields, to see after the cows and horses, and to gather the crops. If their work wasn't done when he got home, whether after work or on the weekends, the boys were whipped with ironing cords or wet ropes. He'd then refuse to let them have supper. Lorraine would fix their plates, cover them with something, put them in their bedroom, and close the door so they could have something to eat.

Many times the boys would see their daddy coming and would lay on their bellies in the field between the rows or climb a tree and sit high in the branches to keep their father from seeing them. When night fell, they'd climb through a window into the bedroom. Always—not sometimes—they'd find their dinner, left by their mother, either under the bed or on the dresser so they could have supper before going to bed. It wasn't a hot meal, but it was better than going to bed hungry.

Godfrey used the boys not doing their work as an excuse to beat or punish them, but in later years, it was found that they sometimes happened to be in the wrong place at the wrong time and would see their dad with other women. If he kept them afraid of him, he thought, they wouldn't tell their momma.

The oldest boy and the third boy, Godfrey, Jr. and Frank, began to hate their father intensely. The oldest girl was sent to Galveston to live with her grandmother, Godfrey's mother, so she could attend the high school there. Lorraine thought there were many more opportunities for her there than in Dickinson. She was determined that her children would have the best education she could afford, since she'd only completed grade school.

Each time Lorraine visited her daughter, Sheryl would beg emphatically to go back home with her. Her grandmother treated her badly and would tell Lorraine lies about the child. If Sheryl tried to defend herself, she was whipped after Lorraine left.

Finally, an older woman who lived nearby came to the child's rescue. She told Lorraine how the child was struck when she spoke when she hadn't been told to, how she had terrible vomiting spells following an argument, and about the cutting sprees her Grandmother Stella would have in the child's presence. Lorraine finally concluded that an education in Galveston wasn't worth her child being sick and miserable. Godfrey, Sr. had learned well. His momma had taught him anger, selfishness, and ridicule.

Randy, the second boy, who Godfrey's mother had accused Lorraine of having by another man because he was darker than the others, was Godfrey's heart. Randy broke a leg playing football, which set up an infection because it wasn't properly cared for. That caused him to walk on crutches for a long time. He wasn't held to chores as strongly as the other boys.

About three years later, Godfrey, Jr., ran away from home at the age of fifteen. Lorraine never heard a word from him for about a year and a half. She had a nervous breakdown and went blind for about four weeks. Sheryl had to drop out of school and stay at home to look after Lorraine and the other children.

Everyone was looking for him, even the Red Cross. No Godfrey. Finally, one day, a gentleman who was in the armed forces came and told Lorraine that he was almost positive that he'd seen young Godfrey in New York a few weeks earlier, trying to join the army. They both knew that Godfrey was too young to get into the service. However, he was a tall and broad-shouldered young man. The gentleman volunteered to check and see if it was true, because if Godfrey had been taken into the army and had lied about his age, he might get into trouble.

Lorraine's hopes began to rise. He cautioned her, however, not to get her hopes up, because he could very easily have been mistaken. When he returned to New York, he checked it out, and it was in fact, Godfrey. He told the boy of his mother's condition and how worried she was, and asked him to write and let her know that he was all right.

Godfrey, Jr. had gone to Jersey City, New Jersey, to live with his grandmother.

She had left Galveston a few years ago and always had a habit of telling her grandchildren, "If your momma and daddy don't treat you right, run away and come to stay with your Big Mother."

Lorraine had repeatedly asked her not to tell them that. That's what the children called her—Big Mother. When Godfrey, Jr. got old enough, he did run away.

Stella never let a soul know where Godfrey, Jr. was. As long as he worked and brought her money, everything was fine, but when he began to want to buy himself things, she told him he'd have to find someplace else to stay.

Lorraine received a letter from the army, wanting her to verify by signature that Godfrey, Jr. was eighteen. Thanking God that she at least knew where he was, and knowing that he'd be better off there than roaming the streets, she signed the papers. A few years later, her third boy, Frank, went into the army.

Lorraine was still working. The fourth boy was getting ready for college. Isaac had a part-time job, so he could help his mom get some of the things he needed to go to college. He wanted to become a doctor. Lorraine borrowed as much money as she could from the bank and called on some of the people she'd worked for through the years to get the rest. Randy had married and Carl, Minnie, and Wynette were in high school. Andrew and Etta were small, and Lorraine, the baby, was still at home. Randy's wife took care of little Lorraine, along with their children, until she was old enough to go to school. She was only two years older than their firstborn.

14. The Reunion, Then Homecoming

One day as Lorraine was leaving one of her day jobs, she walked to the post office, which was only a block from where she worked, to get her mail. There was a letter from Frank. He'd seen Godfrey, Jr. in New Guinea before the outbreak of World War II.

They hadn't seen each other since they were kids. What a glorious time that must have been. They ran to each other, hugging and crying like babies, wondering if they'd ever see each other again.

As the excitement of their unexpected reunion began to decrease, Frank told Godfrey about home and Godfrey, in turn, told of his life since he'd run away. That only lasted a day, for they were sent separate ways. Lorraine began receiving mail from both the boys quite often.

Frank would send souvenirs from New Guinea and write, "One of the big snakes got into our barracks last night, wrapped around one of the guys, and crushed him to death while we slept. We were awakened by his sounds of agony—while very near death. We almost lost another in one of the man-eating plants, but managed to cut him free."

Godfrey, Jr. wrote, "It's unbelievable how Americans are dying here. When the shooting starts, we have to condition our minds to keep moving. You dare not stop to help the fallen soldiers around you until the firing lifts for fear you'll be next. We were running for shelter the other day, and the firing was very heavy. One of the guys fell in front of me, another in back, still another on the side. I felt I'd be next. A million things ran through my mind in a split second. It frightened me so badly that I swallowed my false tooth, but I'm still here. Just need another tooth. Smile—someone must be praying back home. Thank God for that."

Lorraine was saving the money that was customarily sent to the families of servicemen. They urged her to use the money to help take care of the other children, but she refused. She could only think about them having to take care of themselves when they returned without having anything to start with. Besides, she felt that they were going through nightmares of terror for that money and deserved every penny—and more.

It was a Wednesday afternoon in July. Lorraine and Godfrey, Sr. were at work. The children were at home. One of them saw a man in a uniform coming through the hedge opening at the side of the house.

"Brother!" the child cried. "Brother is home!"

A fine-looking young man he was. Six foot two and weighing 200 pounds. He was built and walked much like his mother, with his large shoulders curved into masculinity. He'd only been a child when he left. He brought gifts for everyone, distributed them, and went out the door to see his brother, Randy, who lived at the other end of the five acres of potatoes, corn, and peanuts, just two blocks away. Randy had never gone into the service because of his bad leg.

About thirty minutes later, the children could see their momma coming down the road. She walked to and from work every day. When she got close to the edge of the lawn to turn in, they ran to meet her.

"Momma, brother is home!" they yelled.

The sound of those words made her feel as though she were about to have a heart attack. The son she'd grieved over for so long and hard was home.

"Thank God," was all she could bring herself to say until she ran into the house and saw that he wasn't there.

"Where is he?" she cried.

"He's at Randy's," one of the children replied.

Out of the house she flew. By that time, one of the other children had run ahead to tell Godfrey that Momma was home. Lorraine ran as fast as her tired legs would allow through the field to greet her son.

"Godfrey, Godfrey!"

"Hold on, Momma, I'm coming!" he yelled.

They met midway across the field, holding each other and rocking back and forth while Lorraine sobbed, "Thank God, thank God."

God was truly the one to thank. He'd spared her child through his lonely journey of running away from home, his narrow escapes in combat, and now back to the place where he'd started as a very small child.

I glory in Lorraine's prayers, her faith, and her strength. Thank God.

Oh, that was a glorious day for the Veance family. A little later, Godfrey, Sr. was coming in for dinner in the ice house truck. He had managed the neighborhood ice house for two years and had kept that job longer than any other. He had begun to stay at home more with the family since Lorraine had scolded him with a hot pot of tea, hung a door over his head, and whipped him with a barrel stave while he undressed to take a bath. Even he was glad to see his son. They all sat down to visit over coffee and tea.

A week later, Frank came home. Another glorious day. Everyone was running around like chickens with their heads cut off. Petty (their nickname for Frank) was home, and their big brother, too. Petty was also a handsome fellow. He'd always been rather heavy. He wasn't tall, but was muscular and strong. He was always one to carry out different pranks and games with the children, and they loved it. Little Lorraine never left his lap, unless, of course, she was moving to climb into her big brother, Godfrey's.

Frank was a head chef in the services and could he cook! He loved doing it, too. He relieved Lorraine of a lot of her kitchen duties while he was there. When she got home from work, dinner was ready. Godfrey, Jr. helped, too. They both cooked the best food west of the Mississippi—besides Momma's, of course.

They had about four weeks of total happiness with Lorraine in the kitchen cooking pies, cakes, macaroni and cheese (both of the boys' favorite dish), chicken, eggplant, greens, baked sweet potatoes, everything she knew her sons loved to eat—all raised right there on the property. The boys told of their war experiences and the children and Mom and Dad (they were even cordial to him) told of home and school. There couldn't have been any better medicine in the whole wide world to heal the wounds of worry or the sickness that Lorraine had felt inside than to have her sons home again, but there was a sad day coming. They had to go back. However, it was better to have seen them for a few weeks than not to have seen them at all.

Lorraine prayed at every meal, in addition to the blessing of the food, and every night, thanking God for her sons who were visiting for a short while, and asking that He spare their lives so they could return again, safe and sound.

15. The Rest of Lorraine's Children

Isaac was in college and Carl would go in a couple of years. Lorraine, never having had a child finish college, was very pleased. When Isaac returned each summer (Lorraine couldn't afford to send for him during the year), he'd teach her different terms in German that he'd learned. He often talked about his teachers, roommates, and friends. Isaac liked the small private Methodist college he attended, in Marshall, Texas. He had a job that paid for most of his schooling, which helped Lorraine an awful lot, and *Boy* was she proud of him.

After Isaac's college years came to a close, Lorraine held her head high as he walked across the stage to receive his diploma.

"Thank God," she whispered.

After finishing, he decided to go to California, not pursuing the medical field. He accepted a job as a diesel engineer, graduating to higher positions through the years.

Carl decided to attend the same college as Isaac. He wanted to be a lawyer. He was a happy-go-lucky young man, handsome— and he knew it. Tall, slim, with small features and very flirty, he was a ladies' man. Carl was an average student, passed his courses, but was too rich for Lorraine's pocketbook, and the girls too rich for his.

Minnie was the oldest child at home. She kept house, looked after the smaller children, washed, ironed, and did anything else to keep her momma from having to do all of it when she came home after a hard day's work. She was named after Lorraine's mother and her dad's mother, and she'd inherited some of both of their ways. She was quiet, not having much to say to anyone, and a very hard worker, but when she was angry, you would have thought all hell had broken loose in one blow.

She grew up with at least three of the boys, because there was a big gap between her and Wynette, the next girl. Minnie played basketball and baseball with the boys, raced against them, fought them, and was darned good at all of it—as good as they were, or better. She loved basketball and was an excellent player, as was Carl.

One day they were playing baseball at home on the lawn and Minnie was about to take her turn at bat. Carl decided that he should take her turn, instead. He and Isaac were older and thought they could give her orders whenever they chose to. She politely refused to let Carl take her turn by using his head as a ball. Everyone thought he was dead, but he finally came around.

Minnie got the whipping of her life that day when Lorraine came home, but she never shed a tear. She stood with stern face and stiff body, taking the blows as they came. She never gave anyone the satisfaction of seeing a tear fall from her eyes. She did her crying at night, after everyone was asleep.

Wynette, a little younger than Minnie, would beg, "Cry, Minnie, cry! Then you won't get whipped any more."

Wynette would see her momma coming with a belt or switch and start screaming and crying before she'd ever touched her.

Godfrey, Sr. was mean to Minnie. She did everything she knew to please him, but he never gave her a kind word.

It was always, "Why didn't you iron my work shirt? What did you do with my socks? You don't do anything right."

He never stopped to realize that if it hadn't been for Minnie, many things that were done wouldn't have been done until Lorraine had the time to get around to them. In addition, Lorraine held Minnie responsible for the other children's actions because she was the oldest. She was scolded many times when she wasn't responsible. Minnie couldn't wait for her graduation day. She wanted to get away from home.

Lorraine was getting everything ready for Minnie to go to college. Minnie never said a word, but she was planning to get married to a young man her mother very much approved of who'd recently been discharged from the service.

Minnie was married right after graduation. It was a small wedding, held at the young man's home because Godfrey, Sr. wouldn't allow it to be held in their home. Godfrey, Sr. didn't attend. Minnie was a beautiful bride and seemed very happy, not knowing that, compared to marriage, she'd been living in heaven.

Carl worked all summer at a service station and was preparing to return to college. Wynette was going, too.

"Two at a time, what will I do?" Lorraine wondered.

She knew how hard it had been with just one. Would she make it? She couldn't look for any help from Godfrey. He thought it was foolish to send children to college, especially girls.

"They'll just get married, and I will have spent all my money on them. What would I profit from it?" he'd say.

That made Lorraine work even harder to get her children to college if they chose to go. It never dawned on Godfrey that you don't profit from preparing your children for life. It makes you pleased and proud.

September passed and everything went well. Lorraine would send a little money toward their tuition each month, trying to stay ahead. She sewed late into the night, making clothes for her children and sewing for other people to make extra money.

Godfrey constantly yelled from the bedroom, "I'm going to get an axe and chop that damn machine up if you don't let me get some sleep," as if he didn't buy her new ones when one did play out.

He'd yell and yell until she stopped for the night.

Carl began writing his mom for money quite often. He needed money for books, more for dates, more and more money. November was passing and things were getting harder. Lorraine felt some relief when Aunt Etta's daughter sent money toward her namesake Wynette's schooling.

The second semester was approaching. Lorraine sent both Wynette and Carl money for books and a little spending change, because tuition was due again. A week or two later, Carl wrote to ask for more money.

Lorraine gave up and sent Carl bus fare, one way, a dollar for a hamburger, and wrote, "Come home, Momma."

It almost broke Carl's heart.

He couldn't stop thinking, "I'm in my second year, Wynette's in her first, and I have to go home. Why?"

He got his old job back at the service station and worked a few months before announcing that he'd joined the navy.

Soon it was Etta's turn to go to college. Lorraine tried to convince her to attend the same college where her sister was and where her brothers had gone, but this child had a mind of her own. She wanted to attend Prairie View, where her oldest sister, who had stayed only one week, had gone. She had decided that if she couldn't attend Prairie View, she wouldn't go anywhere. That was where most of her classmates were going.

After much discussion, Lorraine agreed to let her go, but she wasn't there more than two weeks before she wrote Lorraine to come and get her. She hated it.

Upon returning home, she got a job as secretary at the school where she'd finished as salutatorian of her class. She made a good secretary. She was very smart and there weren't many things that she couldn't master after a short while.

Andrew was a year younger than Etta, but wasn't set to finish high school for two more years. He'd been retained in the first grade. He'd only weighed two and a half pounds at birth. Lorraine almost died, and the doctors thought surely he would. They put the baby aside to care for the mother, hoping to save her life so she could raise the rest of her large family.

When Lorraine was comfortable and out of danger, the doctors heard a wee sound, about as loud as a baby mouse. Looking around, they remembered the tiny baby. He was still alive after about five hours.

"Damn," said Dr. Flautt. "If you can live five hours on your own, I will dedicate the rest of my life to keeping you alive as long as I can."

Andrew was named after that doctor, Andrew Flautt Veance, and Dr. Flautt kept his word. He treated Andrew as long as he lived, free of charge, and a lot of treating he had to do. Andrew's feet were turned completely backward. He never had a tooth until he was two years old. He had heart trouble and didn't start walking until he was nearly three.

Andrew nursed from a bottle, even after he started school, and if Lorraine tried to take it away, he'd remind her, "You know, Dr. Flautt said if I want my bottle, to give it to me, and I want my bottle to go to school with me."

Lorraine, knowing what he said was true, would give it back to him. Holding the bottle in his teeth by the nipple and cursing like a sailor, off to school he'd go. Yes, he was a little demon. He was never spanked because of his heart trouble. When he was four years old, he smoked a firecracker on the Fourth of July, blowing all the lining in his mouth out and bleeding like a hog. About six months later, he fell into the well, though he didn't drown. Lorraine let the bucket down and told him to catch hold. The sound of him losing hold and falling back into the water was much like the sound of a frog jumping into the pond from a lily pad.

When Andrew was five, he shot a .38 pistol on New Year's Eve that he'd found under the corner of the house. His dad had hidden it there after shooting it and then going in for dinner. Blood spurted from Andrew's face with each heartbeat. Two years later, at age seven, he was run over by a bicycle. The pedal of the boy's bike was missing and the metal part stuck through Andrew's nose, between the eyes. He almost bled to death by the time Lorraine could get someone to take them to John Sealy Hospital in Galveston.

When Andrew was thirteen, his appendix burst and gangrene set in. He lay in bed all night and part of the next day, complaining of a stomachache. Lorraine decided the next morning that he should see the doctor. He got up that Saturday morning, combed his hair, washed his face, put on his clothes, including his shoes and socks, and walked to the car waiting out front so Lorraine could take him to Dr. Flautt, who immediately sent him to the hospital. Toughest results of a two and a half pound baby I ever saw!

That's not all. One teacher recommended, while Andrew was in elementary school, that he be taught a trade using his hands. He finished high school, went to college, and was called into the army his second year. Little Lorraine was there at the time, a year behind him.

Andrew never got above the rank of private, because he hated that damn army and fought all the time. He came out at the end of three years, got married, and wouldn't you know it, he joined the reserve and was called back two years later. Every time he earned a stripe, it was taken right back because someone would say something he didn't like and he'd start a fight.

He was 5'4" and weighed 125 pounds. He was discharged the second time, still a private first class. He moved from Dickinson to California, then to Ogden, Utah. After Utah, he moved to Dallas, Texas. He was sent to a TB hospital in Tyler, Texas, where a spot on his lungs disappeared after a few months.

With three little daughters now, he decided he was going to get his college education. He enrolled in school, got hit by a train, and received a concussion. Oh, yes, he was still alive. He finished school, went on the next year to get his master's in Family Living, and started working at a University in Pullman, Washington. He later got his PhD in Psychology. He was one tough little piece of leather, well put together, who had a hell of a determination that paid off.

Lorraine, the last of eleven living children, was about to go to college. Her mom had fought a long, hard fight. She had stopped farming and had built two small rental houses after borrowing money from Aunt Etta. However, she paid back every penny, a bit at a time. Some of five and a half acres no longer belonged to her because she had been forced to sell several lots to help her children through college. However, a large portion still remained in her name. She gave most of her children a portion of the land, and only two sold their pieces to raise down payments on homes elsewhere. Three built their homes there and the others still had their land.

Little Lorraine was on her head to go to Fisk University to become a doctor. Her mom insisted that she was too young at seventeen to go off to a school all alone. She'd never attended seventh grade, having skipped from sixth to eighth. She insisted that Lorraine attend school where her brother Andrew was, but he left for the army the second semester of that year, leaving her alone, anyway.

Lorraine was a lover of knowledge. She did well in college, choosing Music Education as her major. She finished college in three years and got married in October of her senior year. It almost killed her mom.

Things were much better for her financially than for the others. She was the last, and all the other children were grown and on their own. She never knew what it was like to work in the fields, to not have shoes, or not have the things she really wanted, for that matter. She, too, was a spoiled little dickens—spoiled by her mom, her dad, as well as, the older children. Even her brother, Andrew, who was just a few years older, sent her money and gifts from Korea while he was in service. That was the glory of being the baby of the family. She was of kind spirit and a giving heart, much like her mom.

Lorraine and Godfrey were suddenly alone at home. She retired from her job at one of the school cafeterias and Godfrey retired from the ice house. All the children were on their own, doing reasonably well. Lorraine had prayed so many times for the Lord to let her live to see her children all grown and able to take care of themselves. Her whole life had been wrapped up in her children and her church.

Lorraine was beginning to have heart attacks, some light and some more severe. She still didn't show her age, even after all of the hard work and worry she'd encountered. She taught Sunday School, worked with the youth, and sang in the choir—her first love. Her Sunday School children had shirts and little dresses made for them from scraps that were given to Lorraine as she sewed for other people. If they didn't have a ride to Sunday School, Lorraine left early, drove around and picked them up, kept them at church, and then took them home. She also made garments and went around in the neighborhood giving them to children in need. She was like her Grandma Kahn in many ways—working hard and helping the needy. Granny Veance was what she was called by all of the children in church and the community.

Every Fourth of July (Godfrey, Sr.'s birthday), all the children who could make it would gather at the old home place with Mom and Dad and their families. When all of them were together, it was nothing but laughs, jokes, teasing, bragging about their children—and don't leave out the eating.

Godfrey and Lorraine were blessed with eleven children. The two oldest Sheryl and Godfrey, Jr., had no children, but Randy had seven; Frank, three; Isaac, two; Carl, five; Minnie, seven; Wynette, three; Etta, four; Andrew, three; and Lorraine, one.

After retirement, Godfrey indulged in fishing—his first love—and playing pool, his second. Lorraine, up until one leg was amputated because of diabetes, of which her mother had been a tragic victim at the age of forty-five, continued to sew, a skill taught to her many years ago by Grandma Kahn. She didn't sew primarily for the money, but because she loved it, and it was a company keeper.

Godfrey, Sr. grew concerned about Momma (as he called her) in his old age. He bought her gifts on every holiday, helped her around the house, planted a garden each year with everything she wanted in it, hung out the clothes and took them in, ran errands, took her back and forth to church, and became even more concerned when she felt bad.

He'd never been a churchgoing person or one to talk about God, but he portrayed many emotional characteristics that would lead one to believe that even Godfrey might have said a prayer or two. When Lorraine blessed the food, which she did at every meal, Godfrey waited patiently with bowed head (but not closed eyes) before he started to eat. She often added a little prayer for someone in the family who was ill or in the hospital. When Godfrey raised his head, his eyes were red and filled with water. Mean, stern, unaffectionate Godfrey, you couldn't fool everyone. You weren't all bad. He would then say, "Good bread, good meat, lets eat," to make everyone laugh.

Lorraine was in and out of the hospital. She was able to control her diabetes until she was about seventy-nine years old. Then it more or less controlled her. One of her legs was amputated, and then the other, but she was still determined to go to church, to cook her meals, to make her bed, to wash the dishes, and to take care of her personal needs while getting around in her wheelchair. She never retired at night without reading her bible for spiritual food.

She died at the age of eighty-six (November 8, 1895–June 4, 1981). Her death was announced at the United Methodist Church annual conference in Houston, Texas. She had worked diligently for years in the Methodist church and was known by many.

Godfrey lived seven years longer. He cut the quarter-acre lawn in front of their house until he fell and broke a hip. From that point on, he was bedridden and senile, until he died of old age at ninety-four (July 4, 1894–June 7, 1988).

Lorraine's life was the result of hard work, determination, and trust in God, for only God could deliver a child, *born and not wanted*, through a life such as hers.

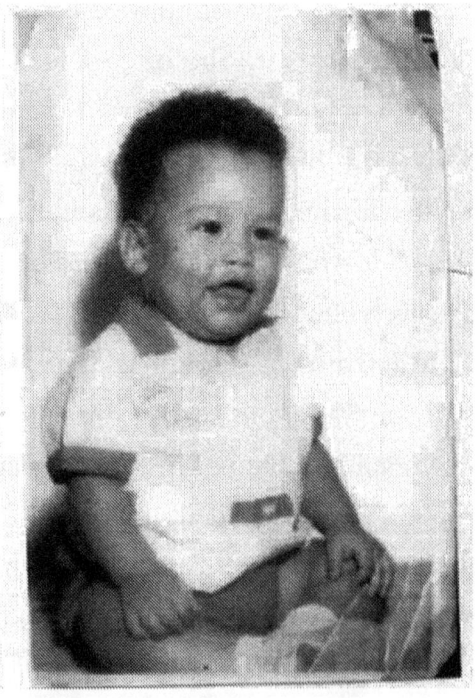

Dr. Kirk, 5 mos.

Dr. Kirk with Mom and Dad

Adam, Austin, Kirk, and Alexander

60th Wedding Anniversary

The Clan

The sisters, in later years.

Lorraine with oldest sons.

Last four children.

Lorraine, Grandmother, and Aunt

Home where Lorraine spent her early years.

(She is smallest figure behind gate.)

Grandma Kahn

Grandpa Kahn

www.ingramcontent.com/pod-product-compliance
Lightning Source LLC
Chambersburg PA
CBHW031230280526
45784CB00004B/1519